CARIBE CARNIVAL

SEP 2024

CONTENTS

Collins

WHERE IN THE WORLD?

7 The Bahamas

8 Grand Cayman

GREATER ANTILLES

9 Jamaica

Cays are sand or coral islands formed over thousands of years from the skeletons of tiny sea animals.

The Caribbean islands lie in the Caribbean Sea to the east of Central America. Altogether, there are 7,000 islands, rocky islets, **coral reefs** and cays.

The islands have a warm, tropical **climate** with a dry season and a rainy season, and the risk of hurricanes from June to November. They have beautiful scenery including mountains and caves, rainforests and jungles, rolling hills, sugar cane fields and volcanoes. The white sandy beaches, warm seas and weather attract millions of tourists each year.

Leeward Islands

6 St Kitts and Nevis

LESSER ANTILLES

5 Martinique

4 St Vincent and the Grenadines

2 Grenada

Windward Islands

1 Trinidad and Tobago

3
Barbados

CARIBBEAN PEOPLES

Carib peoples settled in the Caribbean thousands of years ago. Today, most Caribbeans are descended from European settlers and the people they brought from Africa, China and India to work as slaves on the sugar **plantations**.

From 1500 to the 1830s, European traders and plantation owners shipped in people from Africa to work as slaves on the plantations.

a steel pan band

Tourism is an important industry.

Sugar cane, bananas and spices are grown all over the Caribbean.

There are more than 40 million Caribbeans, speaking English, French, Spanish, Dutch and Creole languages. Caribbean food, dance and music are popular all over the world. Caribbean music includes salsa, reggae and calypso, which is sung and played with instruments, including steel pans, guitars, drums and maracas.

CARNIVAL CELEBRATIONS

In the Christian Catholic Church, people celebrated carnival on the days before Lent, the period of **fasting** leading up to Easter. These days, they're called Fat Sunday, Monday and Tuesday. Fatty foods, such as butter, eggs and meat, were eaten up until fasting began.

Carnival celebrations were introduced to the Caribbean by Europeans. Governors and plantation owners held grand **masquerade** parties, with costumes and masks, dancing, music and song.

Europeans began settling in the Caribbean 500 years ago.

a sugar cane harvest

When African slaves were freed from slavery by law in 1834, they adopted carnival to celebrate their freedom. It grew into a mix of European and African festivals, with colourful costumes, parades with dancing and music, contests and prizes. Carnival celebrates freedom, national feast days or the sugar cane harvest, as well as the last days before Lent.

The word "carnival" means "putting away the meat".

TRINIDAD AND TOBAGO

Trinidad and Tobago celebrate the biggest and oldest carnival in the Caribbean. It begins at daybreak on Fat Sunday, two days before Ash Wednesday and the beginning of Lent. Partygoers paint their bodies with grease, paint, mud or chocolate, and dance through the streets as the sun rises, beating drums and blowing whistles.

On Fat Monday and Tuesday, Mas bands parade through the streets. They're led by the Carnival King and Queen, wearing spectacular costumes decorated with feathers, sequins, beads, laser lights and fireworks.

J'Ouvert (daybreak) celebrations at the start of carnival

Carnival Queen in spectacular costume

PANORAMA COMPETITION

Steel pan bands compete against each other in a grand final. The pans are made from old chemical or oil drums. Dents in the steel create different notes

steel pan band playing in the panorama

when the player strikes them with rubber-tipped sticks. Each band has its own fans cheering it on.

9

GRENADA

Grenada is known as the Spice Island for the spices, like nutmeg and mace, which are grown there. In summer, they're celebrated with a Spice Mas. The Spice Mas begins at daybreak, when the Jab Jab parade through the streets, wearing masks, horned helmets and body paint or oil. As the sun rises, they make way for the parade of Mas bands.

The bands dance and parade with whistles, drums and bells.

The chains and padlocks the Jab Jab wear recall the days of slavery.

People from **parishes** all over the island parade in costume into the capital, St George's, chanting, singing and scattering baby powder.

After the parade it's the Monday night Jump Up, when dancers wave glowing light sticks and dance through to the early hours of the next morning.

MOKO JUMBIE

Masked stilt walkers tower over the Mas parade, dressed in colourful costumes and masks. "Jumbie" means "ghost" or "spirit", and "Moko" may be named after an African god, or the tall Macaw palm tree.

BARBADOS

Crop Over is held in July, and celebrates the sugar cane harvest. It dates back to the 1780s, when slaves working on the plantations held harvest parades. They decorated the animal carts carrying the last of the sugar canes with flower garlands.

Each parish celebrates with parties, goat and donkey races, and contests in cutting sugar canes, drinking coconut milk and stick fighting. Stick-licking, a sport of barefoot stick fighting, was brought by slaves from West Africa.

goat racing on the beach

It ends with Grand Kadooment Day, a public holiday when there's a grand parade of bands, with prizes for the best costumes, the best steel pan band and the most popular song or "Tune of the Crop". Many people go to the beach for a swim or enjoy the fireworks in the main square of the capital, Bridgetown.

ST VINCENT AND THE GRENADINES

The Vincy Mas dates back to the 1780s when French plantation owners celebrated the days before Lent with grand masked balls and parties, ending on Fat Tuesday. Today, it's held in July, attracting thousands of visitors to the islands.

Carnival weekend starts with daybreak street parties and ends on Fat Tuesday with the grand Mas parade in Victoria Park, Kingston.

Children hold a Junior Mas parade, and take part in contests for the best junior steel pan band and Calypso King and Queen.

CALYPSO

Calypso songs have clever and funny words, often making fun of important people or celebrities. They're sung in a pattern of call and response which comes from the songs sung by slaves on plantations to help them get through their working day.

MARTINIQUE

On Martinique, carnival is celebrated over a four-day holiday. Parades and parties begin on Fat Sunday and finish on Ash Wednesday, the beginning of Lent for people of the Christian faith.

People dress in themed costumes for each day of carnival, wearing comical wedding clothes on Fat Monday, red for Fat Tuesday and black and white on Ash Wednesday, to mark the death of King Vaval.

Each town and village creates floats, props and costumes for the parades, and crowns their Carnival Queen, Mini-Queen and Queen Mother.

Bull masks are worn in a Martinique parade.

KING VAVAL

Vaval is a giant dummy who's king of the carnival. He's carried in the Mas parade until the end of carnival when he's burnt on a bonfire.

ST KITTS AND NEVIS

The Sugar Mas on the islands of St Christopher and Nevis, known as St Kitts and Nevis, has been celebrated for hundreds of years. People celebrate Christmas, together with the history of the island peoples.

There are street parties, plays and contests, and a grand parade on New Year's Day. Folk dancers parade in traditional costume, wearing feathered headdresses, masks, and fringed aprons decorated with bangles, ribbons and mirrors.

The clowns are one of the folklore troupes that appear in the parades.

THE BULL PLAY

The Bull Play is only performed on St Kitts and Nevis. It recalls an event that happened on a sugar plantation on the island in 1917. The story is about a prize bull that almost died, but was healed by a vet. An actor plays the bull, dancing around and trying to scare the crowds and make them laugh. The action is set to the music of tambourines, triangles, horns and flutes as the other actors try to tame him.

The actor with the stick is trying to tame the bull.

THE BAHAMAS

Junkanoo is celebrated in The Bahamas on Boxing Day and 1st January, and also in July. The name may come from the French words for "unknown" or "masked" people, or from an African prince called John Canoe.

In the capital, Nassau, spectators watch from balconies and rooftops, or climb trees, to watch the "rush out", a grand parade of dancers and musicians sounding drums, whistles, cowbells and horns. Prizes are awarded for the best bands, costumes and music.

floats decorated with animals

MASK AND COSTUME

Spectacular costumes, headdresses and masks are created from cardboard, paper and cloth, and decorated with bells, feathers, fringes and beads.

a parade in Nassau with dancers and musicians

GRAND CAYMAN

Batabano is the national carnival of Grand Cayman. It's named after the tracks that nesting sea turtles leave in the sand when they crawl up the beaches to lay their eggs.

The carnival is held in May. Stilt walkers, acrobats and limbo dancers join the bands that parade with decorated floats from the public beach to Harbor Drive in the capital, George Town.

Children celebrate the Junior Batabano, with their own parade and music, dance and costume competitions.

Stalls sell snow cones, which are cups filled with crushed ice, flavoured with fruit syrups.

LIMBO DANCING

Limbo is a style of dance which first became popular in Trinidad in the 1800s. It's similar to an African funeral dance called legba or legua. Dancers compete against each other to dance under a bar which gets lower and lower.

The bar is sometimes set on fire to make the competition more difficult!

JAMAICA

In Jamaica, carnival celebrates Independence Day, 6th August. This marks the day in 1962 when the island won freedom from **British Colonial rule** and became an **independent** nation. It's a public holiday and a day for partying, dancing and enjoying calypso music. In the capital, Kingston, there's a Grand Gala parade. Floats carry bands, and dancers carrying flags and wearing the national colours or costumes tell the story of the island's history.

After the parade, many families go to the beach to swim or horse ride, watch dancing contests and eat popular Jamaican foods like fried fish.

FESTIVE FOODS

Stalls sell popular carnival foods such as cornbread fritters, **jerk chicken**, rice and peas, and fried **plantains**.

INTERNATIONAL CARNIVAL

Caribbean communities have brought carnival to many cities around the world. Crowds gather to party and enjoy street parades with decorated floats, spectacular costumes, Caribbean music and food.

In New York, carnival is celebrated at the Labor Day Parade on the second Saturday in September, celebrating the nation's workers. Celebrations begin before dawn at daybreak, when people dress up in costume and throw coloured paints over each other. Crowds gather to watch the parade of floats with bands playing steel pans, drums and whistles.

Labor Day parade

26

The Notting Hill Carnival is Europe's biggest street festival.

In London, the Notting Hill Carnival has been celebrated since the 1960s. For two days over the August bank holiday, the streets of west London are filled with dancers wearing spectacular costumes, the sound of steel pan and reggae music and the smell of sizzling Caribbean foods like jerk chicken and fried plantain.

The Carifiesta is a carnival held in Montreal in July.

GLOSSARY

British Colonial rule   under the rule of the British king or queen

climate   the type of weather in a particular area

coral reefs   sandy or rocky ridges in a tropical sea made of tiny coral skeletons

fasting   not eating food

independent   free and self-ruling

jerk chicken   chicken covered with hot spices

masquerade   a party where everyone wears a mask

parishes   smaller areas within a country

plantains   a type of banana

plantations   lands (usually in a tropical area) where one crop is grown

INDEX

ISLAND CELEBRATIONS!

The Bahamas

Grand Cayman

Jamaica

International

Martinique

Barbados

St Kitts and Nevis

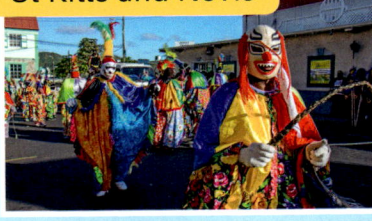

St Vincent and the Grenadines

Grenada

Trinidad and Tobago

31

Ideas for reading
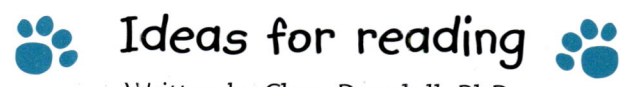

Written by Clare Dowdall, PhD
Lecturer and Primary Literacy Consultant

Reading objectives:
- retrieve and record information from non-fiction
- discuss their understanding and explain the meaning of words in context
- ask questions to improve understanding

Spoken language objectives:
- ask relevant questions to extend their understanding and knowledge

Curriculum links: Geography: place knowledge – Caribbean islands

Resources: ICT, atlas or globe, paper and pencils

Build a context for reading
- Look at the front and back covers of this information book. Read the word "Caribbean" and pronounce it correctly. Locate the Caribbean Sea on a map (ICT, atlas or globe). Read the blurb together.
- Ask children to share what they know about carnivals, and any experiences of them.
- Discuss the costume that the lady on the front cover is wearing and the materials that are used in it. Ask children what this costume tells them about Caribbean carnivals.

Understand and apply reading strategies
- Turn to pp2–3. Model how to use the glossary to find meanings for emboldened words "coral reefs" and "climate".
- Ask a volunteer to read the text on pp4–5 to the group. Check children's understanding of the words "descended" and "European settlers", and discuss the varied heritage of the Caribbean people.
- Challenge children to suggest a definition for the word "plantations". Prompt them to use contextual cues and word knowledge. Help them to check, using the glossary.